HIP-HOP
ARTISTS

DRAKE

HIP-HOP **SUPERSTAR**

BY ALEXIS BURLING

Essential Library

An Imprint of Abdo Publishing
abdopublishing.com

ABDOPUBLISHING.COM

Published by Abdo Publishing, a division of ABDO, PO Box 398166, Minneapolis, Minnesota 55439. Copyright © 2018 by Abdo Consulting Group, Inc. International copyrights reserved in all countries. No part of this book may be reproduced in any form without written permission from the publisher. Essential Library™ is a trademark and logo of Abdo Publishing.

Printed in the United States of America, North Mankato, Minnesota
102017
012018

Cover Photo: Andrew Chin/Getty Images Entertainment/Getty Images
Interior Photos: S. Bukley/Shutterstock Images, 4, 26, 33, 41, 61; Randy Miramontez/Shutterstock Images, 7; Everett Collection/Newscom, 10; Katie Darby/Invision/AP Images, 13; Dennis Van Tine/Geisler-Fotopress/picture-alliance/dpa/AP Images, 14; Kevin Mazur/BBMA2017/ Getty Images Entertainment/Getty Images, 16–17; Rene Perez/AP Images, 18; Photofest, 21; Charles Sykes/AP Images, 23; Featureflash Photo Agency/Shutterstock Images, 29; Leonard Zhukovsky/Shutterstock Images, 34; George Pimentel/WireImage/Getty Images, 36–37; John Steel/Shutterstock Images, 38; Everett Collection/Shutterstock Images, 45; Jonathan Short/Invision/AP Images, 47; Frank Micelotta/Invision/AP Images, 48; Omar Vega/Invision/AP Images, 51; Joe Seer/Shutterstock Images, 55; Krista Kennell/Shutterstock Images, 58–59; Rena Schild/Shutterstock Images, 63; Prince Williams/FilmMagic/Getty Images, 66–67; Christoph Dernbach/picture-alliance/dpa/AP Images, 69; Shutterstock Images, 70; Mark Blinch/The Canadian/AP Images, 72–73; Arthur Mola/Invision/AP Images, 77; Matt Sayles/Invision/AP Images, 78–79, 86-87; Kathy Hutchins/AP Images, 82; Chris Pizzello/Invision/AP Images, 84–85, 89; Amy Harris/Invision/AP Images, 92–93; Ethan Miller/Getty Images Entertainment/Getty Images, 95; Scott Dudelson/Getty Images Entertainment/Getty Images, 96–97

Editor: Brenda Haugen
Series Designer: Laura Polzin

PUBLISHER'S CATALOGING-IN-PUBLICATION DATA

Names: Burling, Alexis, author.
Title: Drake: hip-hop superstar / by Alexis Burling.
Other titles: Hip-hop superstar
Description: Minneapolis, Minnesota : Abdo Publishing, 2018. | Series: Hip-hop artists | Includes online resources and index.
Identifiers: LCCN 2017946869 | ISBN 9781532113277 (lib.bdg.) | ISBN 9781532152153 (ebook)
Subjects: LCSH: Drake (Aubrey Drake Graham), 1986-.—Juvenile literature. | Rap musicians—United States—Biography—Juvenile literature. | Rap (Music)—Juvenile literature.
Classification: DDC 782.421649 [B]—dc23
LC record available at https://lccn.loc.gov/2017946869

CONTENTS

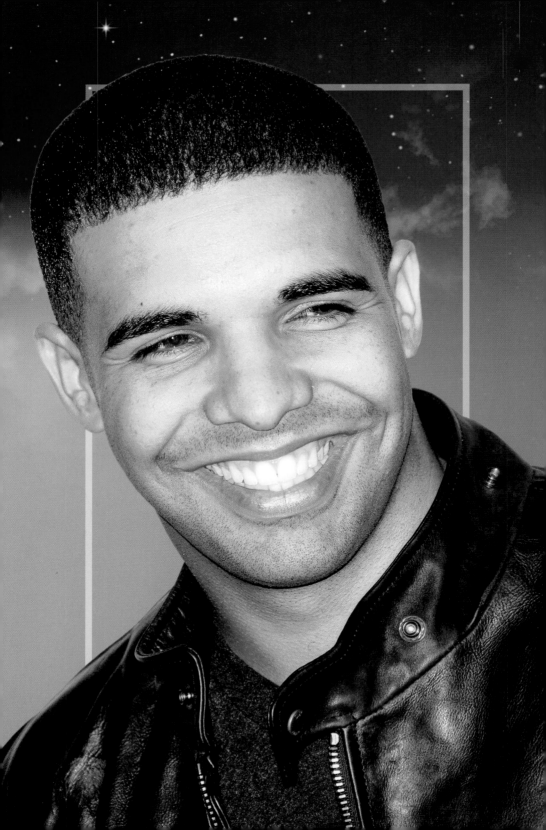

MEETING WEEZY

On a blustery day in November 2008, Drake slouched in a chair at his local barbershop in Toronto, Ontario, Canada. A seasoned actor but then-unknown hip-hop artist, he was busy getting a haircut when his cell phone rang. Rapper James "Jas" Prince, an acquaintance of Drake's, was calling from his car in Houston, Texas, to make a fortuitous introduction.

Jas passed the phone to his friend in the passenger seat. The next five words 22-year-old Drake heard would alter the course of his life forever: "Yo, what's up? It's Weezy."[1]

Weezy, also known as Lil Wayne, was one of the hottest hip-hop artists of the decade. In just a few weeks' time, he would be nominated for eight Grammy Awards, more than any other artist in 2008. Out of those nominations, Lil Wayne would take home four

The connections Drake made as a young man helped build his incredible career.

awards: Best Rap Album (*Tha Carter III*), Best Rap Solo Performance ("A Milli"), Best Rap Song ("Lollipop"), and Best Rap Performance by a Group ("Swagga Like Us").

According to Drake, the idea that Lil Wayne wanted to talk to him was mind-blowing. The two men were worlds apart. Weezy was a bona fide hip-hop superstar. Drake was a relative nobody in the music industry. What could Lil Wayne possibly want from Drake?

LIL WAYNE'S BIG BREAK

Lil Wayne was born Dwayne Michael Carter Jr. on September 27, 1982, in New Orleans, Louisiana. He got his first big break when he was spotted by New Orleans hip-hop label Cash Money when he was 12 years old. The label set him up with an appearance on rapper B.G.'s 1995 debut, *True Story*. Two years later, Lil Wayne joined B.G. and up-and-coming rappers Juvenile and Young Turk to form the Hot Boys. In 1999, at 16 years old, Lil Wayne released his first solo album, *Tha Block Is Hot*. It debuted at Number 1 on the US *Billboard* 200 chart with 229,000 copies sold in its first week of release.[2] *Tha Block Is Hot* peaked at Number 1 on the R&B/Hip-Hop *Billboard* chart too.

A PROFILE ON MYSPACE

Since the beginning of the 2000s, Drake had been trying to break into the music business. He spent hours in his car, drumming his fingers on the steering wheel and writing lyrics to songs he hoped would someday

catch the ear of a record producer or hip-hop promoter. Like many singer-songwriter hopefuls at the time, Drake created a page on MySpace, an early social networking site musicians used to introduce their music to a wider audience and pick up new fans. In fact, it was through MySpace that Drake's music found its way to Jas.

"MySpace had a music explore page at the time, and you could see who was trending by zip code or whatever," Jas said in an interview with music magazine the *FADER*. "I ran across all types of artists on there, like Soulja Boy, but Drake was the one that caught my eye. He was ranked number one or two on the unsigned trending artists list."[3]

Jas knew talent when he heard it. Growing up with music executive James Prince for a father, he had an ear for artists who stood out from the pack. He sent Drake a message. "I let him know who I was and who my father is, and I told him that I wanted to make him famous."[4]

Slowly, the two musicians established a correspondence. Drake began sending Jas sample tracks. In return, Jas sent Drake some music he could rap over, including a track of Lil Wayne's. Although Drake appreciated the connection, he was skeptical of Jas's attention at first. So was Jas's father, who, according to Jas, did not get the appeal of Drake's type of music. Luckily, Jas knew another influential person he could approach who might form a different opinion: Lil Wayne.

NEXT-DAY AIR

The first few times Jas played Drake's music for Lil Wayne in early 2008, Weezy was not interested. He had far more pressing matters to attend to, such as planning an extended tour for *Tha Carter III*. But Jas persisted. Finally, during a drive on that fateful autumn day in 2008, something changed. Jas put on Drake's remix of "A Milli," a hit single off of *Tha Carter III*. Lil Wayne was immediately hooked. He told Jas to book Drake on a flight to Houston. Drake boarded a plane the next day, on November 18.

JAS'S FATHER

During the 1980s and 1990s, most of the well-known hip-hop emcees lived on the East Coast or West Coast of the United States. With prominent record labels in Los Angeles, California; New York City; and Boston, Massachusetts, artists in those cities had plenty of opportunities to be seen, heard, and signed. But hip-hop hopefuls in the South did not have many options, aside from a few labels in Atlanta—until James Prince, Jas's father, came along. In 1986, he founded Rap-A-Lot Records in Houston, Texas. After 30 years in business, the company reigns as one of hip-hop's most important labels. Past and present clients include Geto Boys, Devin the Dude, Z-Ro, and Bun B.

Drake's first face-to-face meeting with one of his idols was not exactly what he hoped it would be. For one thing, it was hot and stuffy on Lil Wayne's tour bus, which was baking in the sweltering Texas heat. Lil Wayne was also in the middle of getting an intricately detailed tattoo of huge wings, one on each side of his body. According to Jas, the star initially gave Drake the silent treatment.

But it did not last long. Lil Wayne invited Drake to join him on his next tour stop, in Atlanta, Georgia. For the next ten days, the two talked shop and collaborated on a few lyrics. Lil Wayne even invited Drake to do a few impromptu rap sessions onstage at some of his shows. On the night before Drake returned to Toronto, Lil Wayne booked time at a recording studio and Drake laid down two tracks, "Forever" and "Stunt Hard."

"A couple of weeks later that got leaked," Jas told the FADER. "That was the beginning of Drake."[5]

"For almost a decade, Drake has been a star and also a curator, the artist most responsible for hip-hop's evolutionary changes and the one most likely to spot the next in line for the crown."[6]

–Jon Caramanica, New York Times, March 20, 2017

HIP-HOP'S WONDER BOY

Over the course of the nine years since he met Lil Wayne, Drake has transformed from a little-known musician with just a few devoted MySpace followers to one of the most sought-after hip-hop artists, with millions of devoted fans around the world. He has garnered a number of awards, including Grammys, MTV Video Music Awards, *Billboard* Music Awards, and BET Awards. In March 2017, he also set a new record for having the most *Billboard* Hot 100 hits in a single week of any solo artist in history, at 24, beating out the Beatles (14) and Justin Bieber (17).

In addition to becoming a musician, Drake made inroads into other creative arenas too. From 2001 to 2009, he played the role of Jimmy Brooks on Canada's cult teen soap opera, *Degrassi: The Next Generation*. Since 2010,

"I went to Houston and met Lil Wayne and that's where [the song] 'November 18th' comes from. . . . That was my first time [there] and the culture and the city was so overwhelming. I felt like I hit Houston and got my swag back. I was single, I was with Wayne and it was Houston, I was going nuts . . . it was [so] fun to me."[7]
—*Drake, Complex, May 29, 2009*

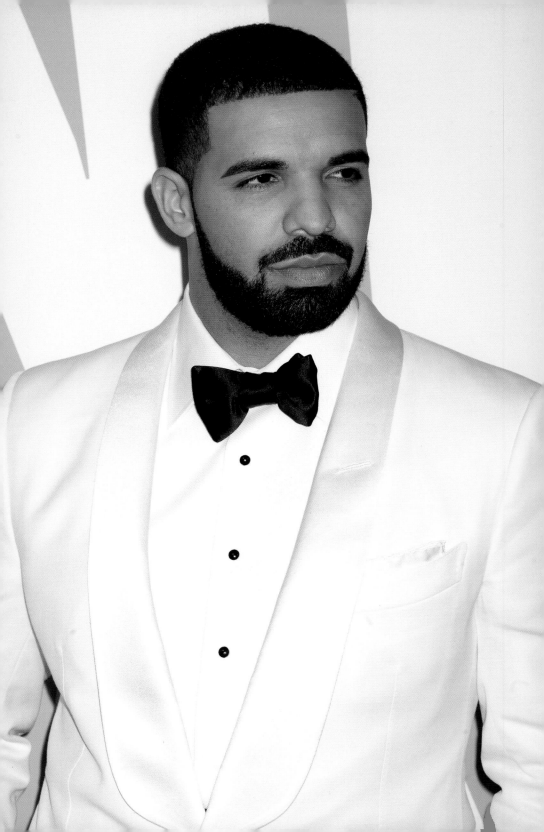

Drake's music has made him a very wealthy man.

he has collaborated on developing a clothing line and become a spokesperson for the Toronto Raptors.

Drake adores his newfound visibility. His attempts to secure fame and fortune have certainly paid off. By 2017, his estimated net worth climbed to $90 million.[8] He ranks fifth on the *Forbes* Five, the magazine's annual list of the world's wealthiest hip-hop artists.

Drake's fans cannot get enough of his music. As for his thoughts on his rise to stardom and his unstoppable drive to succeed, the hip-hop mogul expresses his feelings this way: "What's happening now is meant to be. I don't really celebrate the wins, I don't sulk over the negative. I just keep it moving."[9]

THE *FORBES* FIVE

Every year, business magazine *Forbes* releases a list of the top five wealthiest hip-hop artists in the world. Called the *Forbes* Five, the tally is a way for musicians to see who is on top—and who is not. In 2017, 30-year-old Drake reached No. 5. The others on the list include Diddy ($820 million), Jay-Z ($810 million), Dr. Dre ($740 million), and Birdman, who co-owns Cash Money Records ($110 million).[10]

Chapter Two

CANADIAN ROOTS

Drake's rapid rise to fame and unimaginable wealth began in his early twenties. But the hip-hop star came from relatively humble beginnings. He was born Aubrey Drake Graham on October 24, 1986, in Toronto. An only child, he spent much of his early adolescence in the company of his parents and their friends and relatives.

Drake's parents—Dennis, an African-American man from Tennessee, and Sandi, a white woman from Canada—did not have a large house or flashy cars. But they immersed their son in music at an early age. Sandi grew up listening to soul and jazz. Many people on Drake's father's side of the family held jobs as professional musicians. Dennis was a session drummer for rock-and-roll icon Jerry Lee Lewis. Drake's uncle Larry played bass for the funk band Sly and the Family Stone. Mabon "Teenie" Hodges, another one of Drake's uncles, wrote songs

Despite his humble beginnings, Drake now rubs elbows with other celebrities, such as comedian Kevin Hart, *right*.

Dennis occasionally drummed for rock-and-roll legend Jerry Lee Lewis.

and collaborated with jazz legend Al Green. Dennis's grandmother even babysat Tina Turner when the legendary singer was a child.

The Graham household was known for its raucous family get-togethers. But though the parties were fun, Drake's home life was far from perfect. His parents fought a lot, and Dennis was often in trouble with the law for stealing or drug-related crimes. "My dad was messing up pretty bad," Drake said in an interview in *Rolling Stone*. "He was a mover and a shaker, a hustler: If you had it, he could sell it for you."[1]

Drake's mother grew so tired of Dennis's shenanigans that when Drake was five years old, she and Dennis divorced. Dennis moved back to Memphis, Tennessee. Sandi was awarded custody of Drake, and the mother and son stayed behind in Toronto.

AN OUTSIDER

Drake's childhood in Toronto was rough at first. He and his mother moved from rental apartment to rental apartment until they could afford a permanent place to call home. When Drake was in the sixth grade, they finally settled in the bottom half of a townhouse in Forest Hill, an affluent suburb of Toronto. Sandi developed rheumatoid arthritis,

FATHERLY INFLUENCE

Dennis Graham was raised in Memphis, Tennessee, and taught himself to play guitar, piano, and drums. His first drum "set" was a makeshift tin bathtub. At age 18, Dennis landed his first session job with Jerry Lee Lewis. When Drake was a child, Dennis brought his son along on many of his gigs. Whenever Drake visited his father during the summer, he made regular appearances at Dennis's jam sessions with other musicians.

When Drake turned nine years old, he made a $5 bet with Dennis. "I'm going to do more music than you ever did. I'm going to do more movies than you ever did," Drake told his dad.[2]

In 2009, Dennis finally paid Drake what he owed him. "He did what I always thought I would do," Dennis said in an interview with *Billboard*. "I always thought that I would be that big star, and I never made it. But Drake did it and I felt like, by him doing it, I had made it."[3]

a disease that affects the muscles and joints. Her illness prevented her from holding down a full-time job. Instead, she and Drake relied on financial help from Sandi's brother, who ran the family business manufacturing baby cribs and car seats.

"I only moved to Forest Hill because my mother is an incredible woman who was willing to live far beyond her means for the sake of her family. We rented someone's basement and the first floor. I didn't have some mansion," Drake said in an interview with the *Huffington Post*. "I had a tough time, I definitely had a tough time."[4]

Despite being stretched financially, Sandi did everything she could to make Drake feel capable and loved. She enrolled him

A SIGN OF THINGS TO COME

Drake took lots of artsy classes as a kid—acting, film, and dance. His mother, Sandi, also instilled in him a love for words. She kept four thesauruses in the house at all times just in case he wanted to look something up. "I'd tell him, 'When you're expressing yourself, try and find other words you can use,'" Sandi said.[5]

Her efforts paid off. When Drake was ten years old, Sandi walked into his bedroom and saw him standing on his mattress. He was pretending to be a famous rapper and was spewing out rhymes to a beat. Little did she know that not even ten years later, her son would be rapping into a microphone in front of thousands of adoring fans—instead of into a toilet paper tube.

in tap and ballet classes. She encouraged him to act in youth-theater performances, such as *The Wizard of Oz* and *Les Misérables*.

She also taught him how to find comfort in religion. Drake was raised Jewish, and he and his mother celebrated the high holy days every year. He went to

***Les Misérables* has proved to be one of the most beloved musicals and was even turned into a movie.**

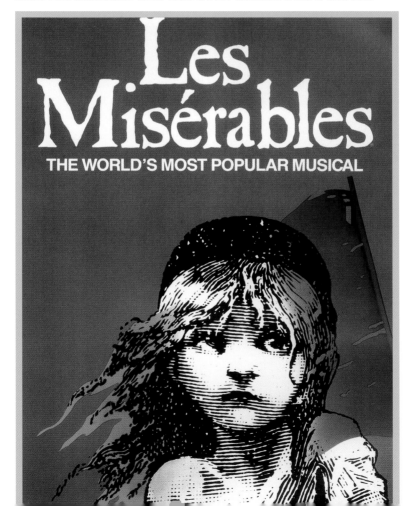

Jewish day school during middle school. When he was 13, he had a bar mitzvah, a ceremony to celebrate a Jewish boy's coming of age.

As a teenager during the late 1990s, Drake attended Forest Hill Collegiate Institute, a public high school in his neighborhood. Though he found some common ground because of his religious beliefs, he mostly felt like an outcast because he was poor and dark-skinned. Many of his classmates whispered racist comments about him when he walked by them in the halls. "Nobody understood what it was like to be black and Jewish," Drake said. "I went to school with kids that were flying private jets. This guy distributes Rolex in Canada, and this person owns Turtle car wax, and this person owns Roots clothing. I went to school with kids who were very fortunate. I never fit in. I was never accepted."[6]

Drake faced a lot of adversity as a kid. Most of the time, he felt different from everyone else. But according to him, the struggle only made him stronger.

A FORTUITOUS MOVE

As would any concerned mother, Sandi worried about her son's exposure to prejudice at school. She also had

DRAKE'S JEWISH INFLUENCE

In the Jewish tradition, it is customary for boys and girls to take part in a ceremony to celebrate their transition from childhood to adulthood. A Jewish boy has a bar mitzvah. A Jewish girl has a bat mitzvah. At each, the teens recite portions of the Torah, the Jewish holy book, in front of their family and friends. Then they celebrate by having a huge party.

In 1999, Drake had a bar mitzvah at an Italian restaurant when he turned 13. Many of his Catholic relatives from his father's side and his Jewish relatives from his mother's side attended. The mix of cultural backgrounds was quite unique.

Drake does not shy away from talking about his Jewish heritage in interviews. In fact, he says it is part of what made him who he is today. His 2012 music video for "HYFR" featured his own reimagined bar mitzvah. In 2016, he even performed at a girl's bat mitzvah in New York City. The set list? "Hotline Bling," "My Way," and "Summer Sixteen."

a hunch that his artistic talents were not being recognized. Hoping that he would have an easier time adjusting in a more tolerant environment, she transferred him to Vaughan Road Academy, a school with a more diverse student body.

Drake thrived at his new school. He made friends. He took film courses and shot an anti-bullying video for a drama class. He became so passionate about acting that he convinced an old friend from Forest Hill whose father was an agent to help him land an audition.

Drake said, "[My friend's] dad would say, 'If there's anyone in the class that makes you laugh, have them audition for me.' After the audition, [my friend's father] became my agent."[7]

For many fledgling actors—even those with agents—the audition process can be grueling. Some actors go for years before landing even a commercial, let alone a minor role on a television show. But not Drake. Soon after he signed with his agent, Drake was asked to try out for a role on one of Canada's most anticipated teen dramas: *Degrassi: The Next Generation*. That audition opened the door to a new beginning. At 15 years old, Drake was already on his way to stardom.

"At the end of the day, I consider myself a black man because I'm more immersed in black culture than any other. Being Jewish is kind of a cool twist. It makes me unique."[8]

—Drake

VAUGHAN ROAD ACADEMY: A HIGH SCHOOL OF GREATS

Drake did not graduate from Vaughan Road Academy. But the school counts him as one of its most famous alumni. Other well-known stars who went to the school include Academy Award nominee Ellen Page, who starred in the movie *Juno*; TV and movie actress Neve Campbell, who had a lead role in the original *Beverly Hills 90210* and was a cast member of *House of Cards*; Arthur Schawlow, who won the Nobel Prize in physics in 1981; Canadian ambassador Klaus Goldschlag; and award-winning novelist Anne Michaels.

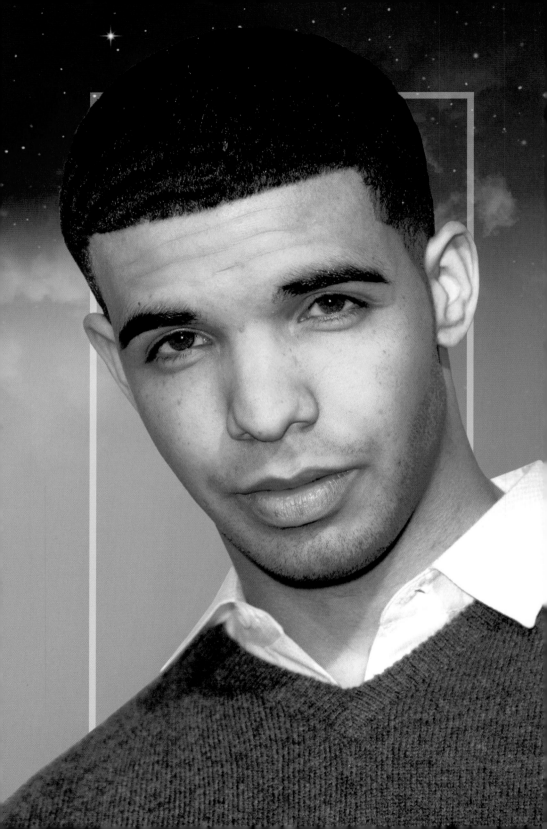

Chapter THREE

DEGRASSI: THE NEXT GENERATION

The year 2001 proved pivotal for Drake. He turned 15—the age at which many boys gain some independence from their parents or guardians, start learning how to drive, and maybe try out their first romantic relationships. But Drake had bigger dreams. He auditioned to play a high school kid on the newest installment of one of Canada's most beloved teen television dramas, the Degrassi franchise.

Created by Linda Schuyler and Kit Hood and filmed in Toronto, Degrassi began in 1980 with *The Kids of Degrassi Street*, *Degrassi Junior High*, and *Degrassi High*. It followed a group of students at Degrassi Community School who grappled with a series of seemingly insurmountable challenges, such as drug addiction, date rape, bullying,

By 2007, Drake was a television star.

teen pregnancy, and racism. The fourth series, *Degrassi: The Next Generation*, was slated to begin airing worldwide in 2001. Casting directors offered Drake the role of basketball player Jimmy Brooks, who gets shot by a rival classmate and spends a majority of the show in a wheelchair.

Accepting the part was not an easy choice for Drake to make. If he joined the cast, he would have to drop out of high school so he could be on set full time. In the end, he decided the payoff was worth the sacrifice. It was his first big acting gig and a chance at fame, and the role came with a salary that would help pay some of the bills piling up at home.

"My mother was very sick. We were poor, like broke," Drake said in an interview. "[It wasn't] that much money when you break it down. . . . A season of Canadian television is under a teacher's salary, I'll tell you that much."[2] Still, the influx of cash helped Drake and his mother stay afloat.

Drake's acting career made him popular with *Degrassi*'s mostly teen viewers.

DRAKE, ON SET AND OFF

Drake had little acting experience when he started filming *Degrassi: The Next Generation*. Of course, he was a teenager and knew how to appear cool and confident. But he also had to learn a new set of rules regarding how to act in a professional setting, such as how to behave on set, when to look at the camera, and how to interact with the other members of the cast without overacting. Luckily, the showrunner and other members of the crew liked Drake immediately and were impressed by his work ethic.

"As soon as he walked in, there was something interesting about him. He had a confidence and a charm, even though he wasn't experienced," said assistant director Stephanie Cohen. "His early episodes weren't the most incredibly

DRAKE'S ACTING CAREER

Drake appeared regularly on *Degrassi: The Next Generation* from 2001 to 2009. He also did other acting on the side during that time. Though none of the roles were as big as *Degrassi's* Jimmy Brooks, Drake appeared on episodes of *Blue Murder* (2001), *Soul Food* (2002), *Best Friend's Date* (2005), *The Border* (2008), *Sophie* (2009), and *Being Erica* (2009). He also did commercials for major brands, including Sears. Fans of *Ice Age: Continental Drift*, which came out in 2012 after *Degrassi* ended, might recognize Drake as the voice of Ethan the wooly mammoth.

accomplished, but he got better. He was open to notes. He would listen."[3]

Drake spent eight seasons on *Degrassi*. In 2002, he and his cast members won a Young Artist Award for Best Ensemble in a TV series (Comedy or Drama). But over the years, in what little downtime he had, Drake's attention shifted to other areas outside of acting. Every time he went to visit his father in Memphis while on break from shooting, he bought more and more music, such as mixtapes by Three 6 Mafia and Yo Gotti. The trips inspired Drake to experiment with writing poetry, rapping, and making his own mixtapes full of songs and remixes of songs by other hip-hop musicians.

Drake also booked time in a recording studio. In 2006, he signed up on MySpace and uploaded some rhymes. That same

A SHOUT-OUT TO *DEGRASSI*

Today, Drake is known more for his musical career than his early days as an actor on Canadian television. Still, he has not forgotten his roots. His stint as Jimmy Brooks is referenced in many of his lyrics. In the song "The Presentation," he raps: "They like, 'Damn, who's Drake? Where's Wheelchair Jimmy at?'"[4] In "Worst Behavior," there is a line that goes, "5 a.m., going to shoot *Degrassi* up on Morningside. For all the stunting, I'll forever be immortalized."[5]

year, he released his first official mixtape, *Room for Improvement*. It sold approximately 6,000 copies.[6]

On September 1, 2007, Drake put out his second mixtape, *Comeback Season*. Andreena Mill, Trey Songz, Dwele, Little Brother, and Robin Thicke were just a few of the artists who contributed lyrics or beats on some of the tracks. The mixtape also included what became Drake's first hit single. Called "Replacement Girl," it is a spinoff of a song written by Brisco and Flo Rida titled "Man of the Year" and features verses by Lil Wayne. "Replacement Girl" was named the "New Joint of the Day" on BET's popular hip-hop TV show *106 & Park*. It earned Drake slews of new fans and attracted the attention of big-name stars, including Jay-Z and Kanye West. It also caught the eye of Jas Prince, the man who eventually introduced Drake to Lil Wayne.

MUSIC ALL THE WAY

In 2008, 22-year-old Drake suffered a blow. He was working long hours on the set each day and then going home to make music. He was exhausted. Then fate stepped in. His character, Jimmy Brooks, was scheduled to graduate from high school. The *Degrassi* producers

Flo Rida is known as a rapper, singer, and songwriter.

suggested that maybe it should be Drake's final season. Though his pride was hurt, Drake was not too surprised by the turn of events.

"That was part of the reason I was kicked off the show," Drake said in an interview with *W* magazine. "Back then, I'd spend a full day on set and then go to the studio to make music until 4 or 5 a.m. I'd sleep in my dressing room and then be in front of the cameras again by 9 a.m. Eventually, they realized I was juggling two professions and told me I had to choose."[7]

Drake chose music over pursuing a future career in acting. Near the end of 2008 and after filming 139 episodes, he left *Degrassi* and graduated to making music full time. With the loss of the

FIRED OR QUIT?

In some interviews with the media, Drake gives the impression that he was fired from *Degrassi* and that he still has resentful feelings about it. But the show's producer insists he was let go, but not fired. "I'm hoping there was just some miscommunication here, because if that's the perception nothing could make me sadder," said co-creator and executive producer Linda Schuyler. "From my point of view, the timing was absolutely brilliant because we knew Aubrey was juggling his music. Not only did we know it, we helped him with it. His character had run its course, so we were nothing but supportive."[8]

Drake poses with some of his *Degrassi* costars in 2015.

acting gig, Drake's access to cash dwindled. He thought about looking for work as a waiter at a restaurant, but fate intervened once more. In November, he flew to Houston to meet Lil Wayne. Drake made such a good first impression that Lil Wayne asked him to join his

Tha Carter III tour. It was an unexpected turn of events that would eventually transform Drake into one of the biggest stars of hip-hop.

BREAKOUT SUCCESS

At the end of 2008, Drake felt full of optimism. He was on the road with one of his idols, Lil Wayne. Weezy was playing occasional shows around the country as part of the I Am Music Tour in support of his multiplatinum album, *Tha Carter III*. Drake tagged along on a few of the stops and sometimes joined Lil Wayne onstage. Wherever Drake went, the crowds seemed to love the former Canadian teen soap star.

"One night, I think in San Francisco, we went up onstage before [Lil Wayne] and the crowd is yelling, 'Jimmy! Jimmy! Jimmy!'" said Jas Prince, who was also on the I Am Music Tour. "We all were looking at each other like, who [is] Jimmy? You got 15,000 people yelling Jimmy and we don't know who Jimmy is but they have Drake's picture on the screen. Finally [Drake's] like, 'That [was] my character on this show called Degrassi in Canada.'"[1]

Drake proved to be a natural performer onstage.

A TELLING COVER DESIGN

The songs on Drake's third mixtape, *So Far Gone*, were fueled by some of the problems Drake was having at the time. He had just left *Degrassi* and did not have a lot of money. He was going through a rocky relationship and was headed toward a breakup. Plus, the question of how he could make it as a hip-hop artist loomed large. The cover of the mixtape reflected all of those issues. Designed by Darkie, a Toronto-based illustrator, the cover featured the outline of a kid standing on top of white letters that spell out "DRAKE: SO FAR GONE AN OCTOBER'S VERY OWN PRESENTATION." As the kid looks upward, a pile of red hearts and money cascade downward on top of his head.

When Drake was not on Lil Wayne's tour bus, meeting new fans, or hanging out with T-Pain, Keyshia Cole, and some of the other rap and hip-hop artists in the I Am Music Tour entourage, he was working hard in the studio on a new mixtape. With contributions from Trey Songz, Peter Bjorn & John, Lloyd, Omarion, and others, Drake felt the project was his best yet.

In February 2009, *So Far Gone* was released under Lil Wayne's Young Money label to widespread acclaim. "Best I Ever Had," the mixtape's promotional single, climbed to Number 2 on *Billboard*'s Hot 100 Singles chart—at the time an unheard-of feat for an unsigned artist. "Successful," a group effort with Lil Wayne and Trey Songz, went gold and made

Rolling Stone's list of "25 Best Songs of 2009." For many in the music industry, it was clear that Drake was not just a fleeting presence on the hip-hop music scene. He was an up-and-coming talent riding the wave of his first big break.

Trey Songz is one of many artists who have collaborated with Drake.

A RECORD DEAL

By the summer of 2009, music industry executives were

paying close attention to Drake. A massive bidding war

erupted among record
labels—each promising
more money than the last
for the chance to produce
and distribute Drake's debut
studio album. At least three
major companies, including
Universal Motown and
Atlantic Records, offered

Drake a large amount of money to sign with them.

Though all the initial figures were not disclosed to the

public, media outlets at the time estimated that some of

the bids were close to $2 million.[2]

As a relatively new player in hip-hop, choosing a label

was a difficult decision for Drake to make. There were

benefits and drawbacks to each. "I am very happy in

my situation now," he told *Billboard* in June 2009 about

his working relationship with Lil Wayne's Young Money

management company. "The most important thing for

me is being around my team—they are stronger than any

label. [But] just know that whatever label we sign to it'll be because they'll add to what we've created on our own."[4]

On June 29, 2009, Drake finally accepted a deal. He officially signed to Young Money Entertainment, with distribution through Universal Republic, a sister company. That same week, he entered the *Billboard* Hot 100 chart with two songs in the Top 10—"Best I Ever Had" at Number 3 and "Every Girl" at Number 10.

To celebrate the occasion—and to get in on the effort to promote big record releases by Lil Wayne, Soulja Boy, Young Jeezy, and other prominent artists—Drake joined the roster for Young Money Presents: America's Most Wanted Music Festival. Slated to begin July 27 in Scranton, Pennsylvania, and last through the beginning of September, the first leg of the America's Most Wanted tour included more than 20 stops throughout the United States and Canada, including shows in Virginia Beach, Virginia; Los Angeles; Vancouver, British Columbia, Canada; and Drake's hometown of Toronto.

The America's Most Wanted Festival did not go as planned for Drake. An injury caused him to miss out on performing in many of the shows. But the time off allowed him to focus on recording his first studio album. It would be his best career move yet.

A DISASTROUS FALL

On July 31, 2009, Drake suffered a setback while on the America's Most Wanted tour. At a show in Camden, New Jersey, he fell while performing "Best I Ever Had" and tore ligaments in his knee. The following evening, Lil Wayne announced Drake would need surgery and would be absent from the tour until he could recover.

Though he was in pain, Drake's attitude remained upbeat. "I embarked on this tour with [an already-injured knee], and due to the events that happened the other night, lord only knows what other damage I have done," he posted on his blog. "On the bright side, I will begin the reflecting and soul searching that it's going to take to make [my first studio] album. . . . I will forever push myself beyond the limits, despite advice and recommendations given, because even with this newfound success, I am still the kid who wanted this more than anything in the world."[5]

DRAKE'S PROMISING DEBUT

Drake released his first full studio effort, *Thank Me Later*, on June 15, 2010. It was full of songs about women and the insecurities that accompany becoming a celebrity. Lil Wayne and rap superstar Jay-Z, as well as Alicia Keys, Nicki Minaj, and Young Jeezy, were contributors. For the most part, fans liked the record's songs, such as "Karaoke" and "Find Your Love." Critics did too. The *Toronto Star* wrote that it "stands out a bit because of the ease with which its author can flit between a reasonably nimble rhymed verse and, more often than not, a

Drake was able to attract seasoned performers including Alicia Keys to collaborate on his first full album.

glorious chorus designed to melt the ladies' hearts."[6] *Thank Me Later* debuted at Number 1 on the American and Canadian album charts and was certified platinum. It sold nearly 447,000 copies in its first week.[7]

Drake went on the road to promote the album. As part of the Campus Consciousness Tour and his solo Away from Home Tour, he played more than 75 shows throughout the United States, Europe, and Canada in 2010 and parts of 2011. Ticket sales from both tours made Drake one of hip-hop's most profitable touring artists in 2010.

Along with an influx of cash, *Thank Me Later* opened more doors for Drake. He started his own annual music

> **Drake quickly joined the ranks of hip-hop royalty.**

festival called the October's Very Own (OVO) Festival. That same year, he was nominated for four Grammy Awards, including Best New Artist, Best Rap Solo Performance ("Over"), Best Rap Performance by a Duo or Group ("Fancy"), and Best Rap Album (*Thank Me Later*).

Drake had become a media darling virtually overnight. "One only has to look at Aubrey Drake Graham's weight class to see how far he has come," wrote *Complex* reporters Toshitaka Kondo and Insanul Ahmed after the release of *Thank Me Later*. "In a short period of time he has already reached a stratosphere where he is grouped with heavyweights like Jay-Z, Kanye West, T.I., and Lil Wayne."[8]

DRAKE'S "SPARK"

In February 2010, Drake appeared in a commercial for the soft drink Sprite. The advertisement promoted the brand's "Spark" campaign, which aimed to inspire teens to express their creativity through music and film. It was the brand's first global marketing campaign and Drake's first worldwide deal. Called "Unleashed," the commercial featured Drake, as well as his producers, 40 and Boi-1da. It highlighted the highs and lows of Drake's studio sessions while recording his hit song "Forever."

The Sprite "Spark" Music Project launched in March 2010. It featured an online interactive music mixer that helped users create their own songs or remix music from Drake with songs from other artists around the world. A month later, the Sprite "Spark" Film Project launched. It provided users with the tools to create their own 45-second animated films.

LOVE AND CONFLICT

By 2011, 24-year-old Drake was working on songs for his next studio album, *Take Care*. In the meantime, he played occasional shows promoting *Thank Me Later* and partied with his ever-expanding fan base after each concert. In January, he was tapped to star in the thriller *Arbitrage*, written and directed by Nicholas Jarecki and costarring Susan Sarandon and Eva Green. But he dropped out of negotiations at the last minute in order to spend more time completing his new album, *Take Care*.

In June, Drake released a sample song on his blog to get fans and the media excited for *Take Care*'s release. Called "Marvin's Room," the single was certified gold by the Recording Industry Association of America (RIAA). It peaked at Number 21 on the *Billboard* Hot 100 and reached Number 7 on the Hot R&B/Hip-Hop Songs chart.

Drake takes the stage at the 54th annual Grammy Awards in 2012.

THE ORIGINS OF YOLO

A few weeks after *Take Care* came out, Drake released "The Motto" as a bonus single. Fans loved the catchy song, especially its reference to "YOLO," an acronym for "you only live once." The phrase immediately became an Internet meme, spreading like wildfire on Twitter, Facebook, Instagram, and other social media platforms. Companies got on the bandwagon too. Walgreens and Macy's even printed the saying on their clothes. But contrary to popular belief, Drake is not the first celebrity to use the expression. Reality television star Adam Mesh, who appeared on the NBC series *The Average Joe*, was the first to say "YOLO" on the air in 2004. He also launched a clothing line with the slogan that same year. Rock band the Strokes released a single in 2006 called "You Only Live Once." Their promotional campaign for the song was "Operation YOLO."

Finally, more than a year after his first album was released, Drake's *Take Care* hit the market on November 15, 2011. The *New Yorker*'s music critic Sasha Frere-Jones called Drake "one of the most interesting stars of the moment" and wrote that the 25-year-old hip-hop emcee's "brilliant" second record was "likely to be one of the year's biggest-selling albums."[1] *Chicago Tribune* columnist Greg Kot also weighed in, saying, "the best of [*Take Care*] affirms that Drake is shaping a pop persona with staying power."[2] The album sold 631,000 copies in the first week.[3]

As in the past, Drake went on the road, playing more than 60 shows to promote the album. His worldwide

Drake seems to connect with the crowd no matter what the venue.

Club Paradise Tour became the most successful midyear hip-hop tour of 2012, grossing more than $42 million.[4] *Take Care* also went on to win the Grammy for Best Rap Album at the 55th annual Grammy Awards.

DRAKE'S PERSONAL LIFE

Judging from album and ticket sales in 2012, Drake's music career had clearly taken off. Flush with more cash

DRAKE'S ESTATE

In 2012, Drake bought a 12,500-square-foot (1,160 sq m) mansion in Hidden Hills, California, a gated community 30 miles (48 km) north of Los Angeles. The $7.7 million compound sits on three acres and includes a 25-seat movie theater, a combination tennis-basketball court, an air-conditioned doghouse, and a stable with stalls for six horses. A huge giraffe statue made of stone perches out front, next to the driveway. Inside, a switch beside a seemingly ordinary bookshelf triggers a mechanism that causes the shelves to swing open and reveal Drake's bedroom and a Jacuzzi. Drake's favorite part of the house is the massive pool. It features a huge slide, a cascading waterfall with a bar, lit-up wading pools, and a few flat-screen TVs.

"Live without pretending, Love without depending, Listen without defending, Speak without offending."[5]

—Drake, Twitter, February 21, 2011

than he knew what to do with, he drove a fancy car and bought a house in Los Angeles. But aside from his songs' references to dating, drinking, and hanging out with unnamed women, information about Drake's love life was slim. Obsessed fans and reporters alike all wanted to know: Was the increasingly famous hip-hop star romantically involved and, if so, with whom?

For years, speculation about who Drake was—and was not—dating after he became a celebrity fueled gossip. Of course, there was Melissa McIntyre, the actress who played Ashley Kerwin—Drake's on-again and off-again on-screen girlfriend throughout *Degrassi*. But Drake and McIntyre were never romantically connected offscreen. Drake also went on a few dates with various stars prior to 2013, including actress Kat Dennings and supermodel Tyra Banks, but neither of those outings turned into anything serious.

In early 2012, rumors began circulating about a romance between Drake and R&B songstress Rihanna. Though neither artist admitted to being in a full-blown relationship, reports of a possible secret romance started popping up in magazines and online. Since meeting on the set of Rihanna's "Pon de Replay" music video in 2005, the two celebrities had been spotted snuggling together at parties and clubs over the years—especially after Rihanna's very public split from her then-boyfriend, singer Chris Brown, in 2009.

Later that June, Drake gave the world a small clue as to what was really going on. He and Brown had been fighting for a long time over Rihanna's affection. One night, at a packed party at W.i.P., a nightclub in Manhattan, the two rivals got into an altercation. Brown reportedly sent an expensive bottle of champagne over to Drake's table as a truce. Drake snubbed the gesture, and a few of Drake's friends approached Brown's table. A fight broke

Rihanna had a rocky on-again, off-again relationship with performer Chris Brown.

RIHANNA'S CONFLICTED PAST

The very public brawl in 2012 between Drake and Chris Brown over Rihanna was shameful for all involved. But the roots of the musicians' competition date back to when Brown and Rihanna first started dating. Their affair was passionate, but violent. In 2009, Rihanna missed the Grammy Awards ceremony. When photos of her face and arms surfaced a few weeks later, the world found out why. The night before, Rihanna had been physically assaulted by 19-year-old Brown—and it was not the first time.

Brown was arrested and charged with battery. He was sentenced to six years probation and community service. Though the couple broke up right after the confrontation, their on-again, off-again relationship continued. A little more than three years after the attack, they reunited—right around the time Drake's feelings for the R&B singer were at their peak.

out, and bottles were thrown. Many people were injured, including NBA star Tony Parker, who filed a lawsuit. W.i.P. also lost its liquor license.

The Chris Brown incident at W.i.P. tarnished Drake's image. But it was not the last major public dispute he would get involved in that year—or in the future. Constantly in the limelight and wealthier than he had ever been in the past, Drake was more susceptible than ever to controversy. Because of his fame, he also received more attention from women. During the next few years, his name would be linked to lots of starlets—and just as

in the past, Drake kept the full truth about what happened behind closed doors under wraps.

LEGAL TROUBLES

Drake aims to steer clear of controversy. But despite his best efforts, he has been involved in some bitter disputes in his short music career. In 2012, former girlfriend Ericka Lee sued Drake, claiming she cowrote his hit song "Marvin's Room" and deserved royalties. The lawsuit was settled out of court in 2013.

The estate of the jazz musician Jimmy Smith sued Drake in 2014 for $300,000.[6] They argued that Drake sampled "Jimmy Smith Rap," Smith's 1982 single, without asking permission to do so. In 2017, a judge ruled in Drake's favor, and the case was dropped.

Also in 2014, Drake got into a dispute with Rappin' 4-Tay. The rapper claimed that Drake's verse on YG's "Who Do You Love" was nearly identical to some of the lyrics from the 1994 Rappin' 4-Tay song "Playaz Club." Drake settled the dispute by paying out $100,000 later that year.[7]

LOVE IS IN THE AIR . . . OR IS IT?

In the years following Drake's arrival on the hip-hop scene, he developed a reputation as being somewhat of a ladies' man. In addition to Rihanna, plenty of other women—some famous, others not—captured his eye and interest. Since he and Nicki Minaj were on tour together as part of Lil Wayne's Young Money entourage in 2009, the heat between the two musicians grew intense. In 2014, they appeared together in Minaj's steamy music video for "Anaconda." According to fans and news outlets, their mutual physical attraction was obvious.

Aside from Minaj, Drake's name has been linked to dozens of other women. Some of the leading ladies include Serena Williams, Taylor Swift, Hailey Baldwin, Zoe Kravitz, and Jennifer Lopez. But despite his fans' insatiable appetite for gossip and the media's coverage of Drake's hypothetical love life in tabloids such as *TMZ*, *People*, and *US Weekly*, the question of whether Drake has—or will have—a serious long-term girlfriend has yet to be answered.

"So, are they or aren't they an item? It's the question fans of Drihanna/Aubrih have been asking since Drake and Rihanna first sparked rumors of a potential love connection—which, let's be honest, isn't particularly hard to believe considering the pair's undeniable chemistry, made apparent in their live performances, song collaborations and subsequent music video cameos."[8]

—Grace Gavilanes, People, *February 22, 2017*

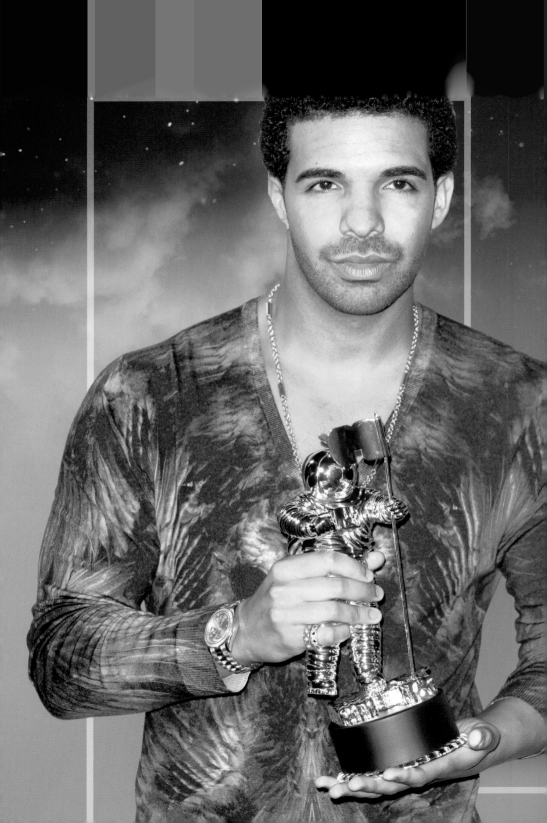

RISING TO THE TOP

When you are famous, staying out of trouble—and out of the tabloids—can be tricky. Making amends can prove even harder. Drake was still stewing over the brawl with Chris Brown at the end of 2012. "It's embarrassing, the amount of media coverage," he later told *GQ*. "Two rappers fighting over the woman. He's not even a rapper, but still, it's the last way you want your name out there. It distracts from the music."[1]

Despite the controversy, Drake managed to end 2012 on a high note. On September 6, he bested Kanye West, Nicki Minaj, Watch the Throne, and Childish Gambino to win Best Hip-Hop Video at the MTV Video Music Awards for his song "HYFR." "The Motto" took the Number 4 spot on *Billboard*'s year-end Top R&B/Hip-Hop Songs chart. *Take Care* was the *Billboard* Number 1 R&B/

Drake earns an award at the 2012 MTV Video Music Awards.

Drake shows off his stylish side at the 2013 Grammy Awards.

Hip-Hop album. *Billboard* also named Drake the 2012 Top R&B/Hip-Hop Artist.

With all the acclaim, Drake felt even more pressure to stop obsessing over love and get back into the studio to record his next album. "I've made a lot of music about love being the only thing I'm missing. . . . If I wasn't doing this, man, and I was back home in Toronto, and I had my job that kept me in the city, my girl would be my life," he said. "[But] I just have new goals, new places to go, new people to meet. I live off a different high point every day."[2]

> "For a rapper as well known as Drake, there remains an essential element of mystery about him. For one so open, there's a distance, and he prefers it that way. But then there's something beneath the exterior that reveals itself with urgency in conversation: Drake's raw ambition."[3]
> —Michael Paterniti, GQ, *June 18, 2013*

Alternating between the built-in recording studio at his house in Los Angeles and four recording studios back in Toronto, Drake and longtime friend and music producer Noah "40" Shebib worked for weeks on end creating and mixing the tracks for Drake's third studio album. Everything had to be perfect. Their goal was to switch gears

OVO SOUND

Drake's first two studio albums were released under different labels—Young Money, Cash Money, Universal Motown; and Young Money, Cash Money, Universal Republic. But ever since he started making music, Drake had daydreamed about starting his own label. That goal became a reality in 2012. With the help of Shebib and tour manager Oliver El-Khatib, Drake founded OVO Sound, a record label based in Toronto and distributed by Warner Bros. Records. OVO Sound released Drake's third studio album, *Nothing Was the Same*. Today, the label represents PartyNextDoor, Majid Jordan, Roy Woods, and others.

from Drake's long-winded raps about girls and money and write genre-bending hits that could be played on heavy rotation on the radio and rock the loudspeakers at clubs.

"When I'm writing, I'm thinking about how the songs are going to play live. Fifty bars of rap don't translate onstage," Drake said. "That's why on this album I've been trying to condense my thoughts to sixteen-bar verses. There's something to be said for spacing out the lines, to infiltrate people's minds."[4]

NOTHING IS THE SAME

Hot on the heels of his first Grammy win in February 2013 for *Take Care*, Drake released the first single in advance of his new album, titled "Started from the Bottom." A few

Many stars go on Jimmy Fallon's talk show to promote their music.

months later, in August, he released a second single, "Hold On, We're Going Home," which peaked at Number 1 on the *Billboard* Hot R&B/Hip-Hop Songs chart. The video for the song earned him a second MTV Video Music Award the following year. In September, he plugged his third single, "Too Much," in a guest appearance on *Late Night with Jimmy Fallon*. Drake also appeared on the cover of a number of magazines, including *GQ* and *Billboard*.

Finally, Drake's third album, *Nothing Was the Same*, was ready to go. On September 24, 2013, it was released. It debuted at Number 1 on the US *Billboard* 200 list, and it sold 658,000 copies in its first week.[5] It also topped the charts in Canada, Denmark, Australia, and the United Kingdom.

As always, Drake launched a massive promotional campaign to get his fans pumped. In January 2014, he hosted and appeared as a musical guest on *Saturday Night Live* for the first time. He also went on the road for the Would You Like a Tour? beginning in October 2013 and stretching until March 2015. The tour featured supporting acts such as Future, Miguel, and PartyNextDoor. By the end of the run of more than 57 shows, Drake had amassed an estimated $46 million in ticket and merchandise sales. More than 600,000 fans flocked to see him perform.[7] For Drake, it was clear nothing *was* actually the same—and his fame only seemed to be growing.

A YEAR OF SURPRISES

During the next year and a half, Drake continued doing what he did best: touring and making music. On the eve of Super Bowl XLVIII in 2014, he headlined a private party for Time Warner Cable's REVOLT, hosted by Diddy. Drake also played several shows in the United Kingdom as an extension of the Would You Like a Tour? in March. Four months later, his now world-famous OVO Festival in Toronto kicked off another streak of shows throughout the

DRAKE HOSTS *SNL*

On January 18, 2014, Drake hosted *Saturday Night Live* for the first time. In addition to performing "Hold On, We're Going Home" and "From Time" as the night's musical guest, he also appeared in nearly every comedy sketch. His opening monologue was a funny take on his bar mitzvah. He also starred in a skit called "Before They Were Stars" that made fun of Lil Wayne and Jay-Z.

"It took Drake only one try to become one of *Saturday Night Live*'s best hosts," wrote CNN columnist Breeanna Hare.[8]

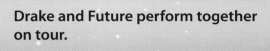

United States that continued into December, including a mini Jungle Tour with Future. But lest Drake fans think the hip-hop star was resting on his laurels and just having fun on the road, 2015 held a few surprises. On February 13, Drake put his fourth mixtape on iTunes without any fanfare or prior announcement. Fans were thrilled. *If You're Reading This It's Too Late* sold more than one million copies that year, making Drake the first artist in any genre to do so in 2015.[9] It was his fourth project to go platinum, after *Nothing Was the Same*, *Take Care*, and *Thank Me Later*.

Drake followed that up by releasing another mixtape to the masses on September 20. It was a collaborative effort with Future that was mixed and recorded in Atlanta in less than a week. *What a Time to Be Alive* debuted at Number 1 on the *Billboard* 200, making Drake and Future the

Drake breaks barriers by performing all over the world.

first hip-hop artists to have two projects reach the top spot in the same year since 2004.

"It's a little soundtrack for people that need it right now," Drake told *Rolling Stone*. "When you get around Future, it's like a vortex, that guy can outwork anybody right now. . . . It's tough to see someone do four, five songs in one night and not try to match it."[10]

By the end of 2015, Drake had surpassed his own expectations. He appeared on the cover of music magazine the *FADER*—a huge honor. But he also had another surprise up his sleeve. In just a month's time, he would announce his latest endeavor: a fourth studio album.

IN DUBAI

On March 14, 2015, Drake played a concert in Dubai, United Arab Emirates. He became one of only a small number of hip-hop artists to have done so, including Eminem and Jay-Z. More than 15,000 fans showed up to see the show. Wearing baggy white jeans and a white T-shirt, he wowed the audience with songs such as "Trophies" and "Started from the Bottom."

"Drake's sweet croon, his secret weapon, was [on] display in 'Best I Ever Had,' which kept the track just on the right side of racy. 'The Motto' also went down a treat, with those big stonking beats sounding so large that those in the front rows could feel them pounding on their chests," wrote the *National* columnist Saeed Saeed the day after the show.[11]

NEW ARTISTIC VENTURES

For Drake, 2016 was a landmark year. In January, he announced he would release his fourth studio album later that spring. In October, the star turned 30—a milestone birthday. His music career was better than it had ever been before.

But by that time, Drake was not just a hip-hop megastar. During the last few years, he had collaborated on projects in other creative fields and solidified the Drake brand. Aside from starting OVO Sound in 2012, he developed a relationship with Apple Inc. in 2015. After the launch on June 30 of Apple Music, a worldwide music and video streaming service developed by the company, Apple announced Drake would be one of the leading faces of the platform. He was hired on as the host of OVO Sound Radio, a weekly radio show airing on Beats 1 that introduced listeners to the newest hip-hop and rap music.

Drake is known as a fashionable star, even when he is looking casual.

A big fan of professional basketball, Drake attended many events when Toronto hosted the 2016 NBA All-Star Game.

The lucrative deal went through for the reported sum of $19 million and initially gave Apple exclusive rights to Drake's music during a release.[1]

That same month, Drake was asked by esteemed art auction house Sotheby's to help curate their exhibition of contemporary works by African-American artists. His role

"HOTLINE BLING"

On July 31, 2015, Drake released the lead single in advance of his upcoming fourth studio album. Called "Hotline Bling," the song featured snappy lyrics such as "You used to call me on my cell phone / Late night when you need my love." The song premiered on Beats 1 and OVO Sound Radio. "The bump and shuffle of the beat, muted and intimate, is gorgeous and aching," Jayson Greene wrote in a review in *Pitchfork*.[2]

In October, Drake made a music video for the song. It was shot inside an exhibit featuring the work of James Turrell, a visual artist known for his experimentation with natural and artificial light. The video went viral. On the day of its release, the video was tweeted more than 324,000 times and the hashtag #hotlinebling was used more than 146,000 times on Instagram.[3] Drake's goofy dance moves spawned several Internet memes starring celebrities ranging from US Senator Bernie Sanders to SpongeBob.

was to provide a soundtrack for visitors as they walked through the New York gallery and looked at some of the pieces. The show, called "I Like It Like This," featured 56 works by some of the most famous names in the art world. Some of Drake's pairings included Lorna Simpson's *Portrait* (with Rihanna's "B**** Better Have My Money"), Jean-Michel Basquiat's *Black* (with Yo Gotti's "Gangsta Party"), and Tony Lewis's *LOLO* (with Chief Keef's "Faneto").

Drake also dabbled in the retail industry. In 2011, he and his tour manager, Oliver El-Khatib, launched the OVO—October's Very Own—clothing line, which sold T-shirts, sweatshirts, and other Drake-related merchandise. In later years, OVO branched out and teamed up with retail giants such as Canada's Roots clothing store and London high-fashion retailer Brown's to create items such as tour jackets and fancy winter coats. OVO even designed a few iterations of Air Jordan shoes for Nike and a Jordan Brand flight suit.

When asked about his attitude toward creating fashion trends, Drake told *Complex*, "I want to give you a product. I want to give people a piece of myself, that's me, that's all I have. I'm just trying to find a way to do it properly."[4]

A NEW STUDIO ALBUM

With many side projects going on at all times, Drake was a busy man. But he never lost sight of his main goal: to make music for his fans and stretch the boundaries of hip-hop. On April 29, 2016, he released

"We really wanted a key tastemaker, someone in black American culture who everyone's got their eyes on. [He was] really hands on with everything, from the catalogue to the design of the invitation to the song choices to the DJ for the opening party. [He was one of the] easiest curators I've worked with by far."[5]

—*Sotheby's contemporary art specialist Jacqueline Wachter, FADER, April 30, 2015*

Drake shows love to his hometown and its sports teams.

his long-awaited fourth studio effort, *Views*. The album was an homage to his hometown, Toronto. In an interview leading up to its release, Drake was asked if he took for granted his ability to connect with listeners now that he was famous. Drake was appalled by the idea.

"I've never felt like, 'Oh, people will bite at anything that's Drake,'" he told the *FADER*. "I'm just not that guy. I don't feel that way about any of my music. . . . If it didn't connect, I would have a huge problem. . . . Like I'm *trying*. I'm really trying to make music for your life."[6]

Drake need not have gotten worked up. Though critics were mixed on the album overall, fans could not get enough of it. *Views* sold 852,000 copies in the

DRAKE'S CONTROVERSIAL IMAGE

In 2016, *GQ* named Drake "one of the most stylish men alive," saying "the king of cozy style can do it all" and calling his jackets and coats "the best outerwear wardrobe since Diddy was rocking furs on a daily basis."[7] But not everyone is thrilled about Drake's apparel. The star has gotten flak from fans for wearing ultra-expensive clothing—particularly pieces that barely anyone can afford. For example, in his popular "Hotline Bling" video, Drake sported a Moncler Maya Jacket ($1,150), an Acne Studios Jayden turtleneck ($400), and OVO sweatpants ($128).

first week—a personal best sales week for Drake, the biggest for any album in 2016, and the largest for a male artist in more than three years.[8] The album's songs were streamed a record-breaking 245.1 million times in the United States during the week of its debut.[9]

One song off the album did particularly well. "One Dance" became Drake's first Number 1 single in Canada, and his first Number 1 as a lead artist on the US *Billboard* Hot 100. The song was also the streaming service Spotify's most streamed song ever, with more than 882 million plays as of October 2016.[10]

AWARDS SEASON

Throughout 2016, Drake traveled around the world playing shows, including the Summer Sixteen Tour with Future and a headlining performance at the 2016 iHeartRadio Music Festival. Then it was time for awards season. Drake had been tapped for several awards

TORONTO: DRAKE'S MUSE

Drake dedicated his fourth studio album to Toronto. The city is one of the most diverse in the world. Fifty-one percent of Toronto's population is foreign-born. People hailing from approximately 230 countries around the world call the city home. Drake's fourth studio album was originally called *Views from the Six* before it was shortened. The "Six" stems from the fact that one of Toronto's area codes is 416. Toronto also used to be made up of six areas: Old Toronto, Scarborough, East York, North York, Etobicoke, and York.

"Smack in the middle of *Views*, Drake does it: He drops a nearly perfect song ["Controlla"]. Suddenly, it doesn't matter that his fourth studio album is overly dramatic, too braggy, so bloated, and a little delusional. Blissed-out, sun-kissed chords shimmer like a mirage, [and] Drake's voice sounds like he's on vacation."[11]
—*Rebecca Haithcoat*, SPIN, *May 3, 2016*

in the past. But because of his increasing fame and proven talent, he was starting to receive more nominations than ever before. At the 2016 BET Hip-Hop Awards in October, he was nominated 14 times, the most earned by any artist that year. He won two of those awards: Album of the Year (for *Views*) and Best Hip-Hop Video (for "Hotline Bling").

Drake also did well at the Grammy Awards, which were held in February 2017. He was nominated eight times. He did not win Record of the Year, Album of the Year, or Best Rap Album for *Views*. But he did pick up Best Rap/Sung

Performance and Best Rap Song for "Hotline Bling."

But none of this success prepared Drake for what was about to come next. It would turn out to be one of the most stunning occurrences of the season. He was about to pull off one of the most incredible feats of his career.

GRAMMY SNUB

Drake picked up two awards at the 59th annual Grammy Awards: Best Rap/Sung Performance and Best Rap Song for "Hotline Bling." But the hip-hop star was miffed by the event. He was confused by the fact that his music was considered rap instead of pop. He was also annoyed by the fact that most of the African-American artists who were nominated had been plunked into "urban categories."

Drake said: "I won two awards last night, but I don't even want them, because it feels weird for some reason. It just doesn't feel right to me. . . . [They want to] pacify me by handing me something, putting me in that category, because it's the only place you can figure out where to put me."[12]

BREAKING RECORDS

On May 21, the 2017 *Billboard* Music Awards show was held in Las Vegas, Nevada. Unlike the Grammys, which are voted on by Recording Academy members, the *Billboard* awards are doled out to stars with the highest number of album sales, song streams, and intake of tour revenue in a given year. For Drake fans, it was certainly an evening to remember.

The star-studded night opened with Drake's old flame Nicki Minaj singing a four-song medley amidst a cloud of smoke and flashing lights. Dressed in a mesh and black leather body suit with silver metal and glitter accents, Minaj blew the audience away with powerful renditions of "No Frauds," "Light My Body Up," "Swalla," and "Regret in Your Tears." Lil Wayne, David Guetta, and Jason Derulo accompanied her as surprise guests.

Drake poses with the hardware he won at the 2017 *Billboard* Music Awards.

Nicki Minaj performs at the 2017 *Billboard* Music Awards.

Minaj was coming off the high of breaking a world record just two months earlier. Among female artists, she had surpassed the legendary Aretha Franklin for having

the most hits on *Billboard*'s Hot 100 chart. Minaj had 76.
The rest of the top five included Franklin, with 73; Taylor
Swift, with 70; Rihanna, with 58; and Madonna, with 57.

But Minaj was not the only record-breaker present at the awards ceremony that evening. Alongside EDM-pop duo the Chainsmokers, Drake picked up a whopping 22 nominations in advance of the show. Some of his nominations included Top 100 Song ("One Dance"), Top Rap Song ("Fake Love"), Top R&B Collaboration ("Come and See Me"), and Top Radio Songs Artist.

The energy in the air was unmistakable that night. Diddy, Bruno Mars, Beyoncé, Vanessa Hudgens, and 2017 *Billboard* Music Awards ICON Award recipient Cher were just a few of the big names who graced the stage. People around the world were all asking the same question: Who would win the most awards?

AN ELECTRIC PERFORMANCE

Before the televised portion of the 2017 *Billboard* Music Awards even started, Drake had already picked up 10 awards. Some

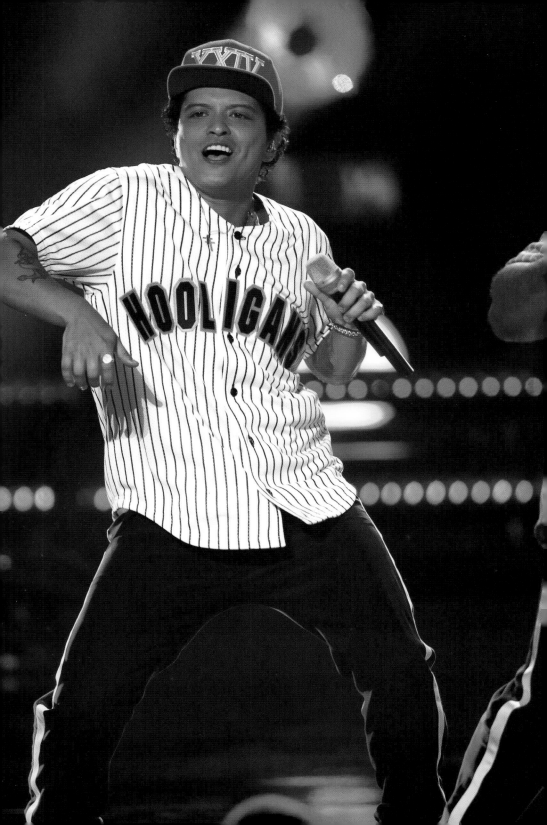

Drake accepts the award for top *Billboard* 200 album for *Views*.

included Top *Billboard* 200 Artist, Top Hot 100 Artist, Top Song Sales Artist, Top Streaming Songs Artist, and Top Rap Artist. After the television cameras turned on and the world tuned in, he won two more: Top Male Artist and Top *Billboard* 200 Album, for *Views*. He had to get just one more to break British singer Adele's 2012 record of 12.

Drake needed to win Top Artist. The competition for that award was stiff. The other nine contenders were among the hottest names in the music business: Beyoncé, Justin Bieber, the Chainsmokers, Ariana Grande, Shawn Mendes, Rihanna, Twenty One Pilots, the Weeknd, and record-holder Adele.

Tension was high. But before the winner was

DRAKE GETS HIS FLIRT ON

In his lyrics, in his music videos, and on tour, Drake has earned a reputation for being a flirt. His performance at the 2017 *Billboard* Music Awards was no different. In his acceptance speeches for two awards, he mentioned one potential future flame as well as one from the past. During his speech for his Top 200 album win for *Views*, Drake flirted with the awards show cohost, actress Vanessa Hudgens. "Vanessa Hudgens, you look incredible tonight," he said. When he accepted the Top Artist award, Drake said: "I want to say, Nicki Minaj, I'm so glad we found our way back because I love you and I could never, ever, ever see it any other way."[1]

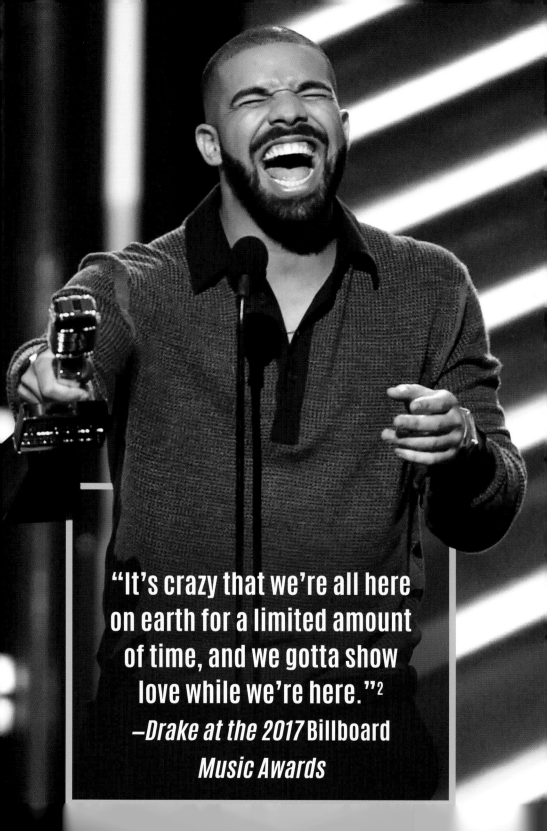

"It's crazy that we're all here on earth for a limited amount of time, and we gotta show love while we're here."[2]
–Drake at the 2017 Billboard Music Awards

revealed, Drake surprised the audience by belting out an electric rendition of his song "Gyalchester." Dressed all in white and standing atop a platform in the middle of the iconic Fountains of Bellagio in front of Las Vegas's Bellagio Resort and Casino, Drake delivered an explosive performance. As water jetted into the air, fireworks exploded all around him. Jaws agape and watching from inside the T-Mobile Arena, the crowd went wild at the spectacle.

Soon, it was time for the big event, and the last award of the evening, Top Artist. Prince Michael Jackson, the eldest child of pop legend Michael Jackson, took the stage. A hush fell over the audience. Finally, he spoke. "I'm honored to be here on a show that meant so much to my father and

THE FOUNTAINS OF BELLAGIO: A PERFORMANCE SPACE?

When Drake stepped onto the stage in the middle of the Fountains of Bellagio, people across the world were floored by his performance. But Drake was not the first superstar to sing and dance in the middle of the 375,000-square-foot (35,000 sq m) aquatic monument. Britney Spears had sung "I'm a Slave 4 U" there 15 years earlier during the 2002 *Billboard* Music Awards. The man-made lake holds 22 million gallons (83 million L) of water and costs an estimated $10,000 to $15,000 per night to run.[3]

made him the recipient of many awards," Jackson said before presenting the winner with the top prize. "He has broken the record for the most Billboard Music Awards in a single year . . . Drake!"[4]

The crowd erupted in screams and applause. Drake had done it. He had won Top Artist of 2017 and broken Adele's record. He took the stage with his friends, his colleagues, and his father, who was dressed in a vibrant purple suit. Drake raised his thirteenth *Billboard* award—a gleaming gold statue of a microphone—in the air and smiled.

A BLOCKBUSTER CAREER

The year 2017 saw Drake experiencing an all-time career high. In the spring, he released *More Life*. A compilation playlist of 22 songs that all appeared

AN ELITE GROUP

In 2017, Drake broke Adele's record for winning the most *Billboard* Music Awards in a single evening. The feat also earned him an entry into a select group of musicians who also picked up double-digit wins in past years. Aside from Drake and Adele, there are only two other musicians in the group. The first artist to do so was Whitney Houston, in 1993, for her album *The Bodyguard* and her song "I Will Always Love You." In 2004, Usher followed, with his album *Confessions* and his Number 1 song "Yeah!"

Lil Wayne held the record as the soloist with the most Hot 100 hits until Drake surpassed him.

on the *Billboard* Hot 100, *More Life* earned him the record

for most Hot 100 hits by a solo artist in the history of the

chart, with 154. Lil Wayne (135), Elvis Presley (108), James

Brown (91), and Jay-Z (87) took the other four spots in the top five on the list. Only the cast of the television show *Glee* had more, with 207.[5]

"When you get right down to it, Aubrey Graham is a playlist—a true pop visionary who's always a fan at heart, an omnivore with a raging appetite for his next favorite sound."[6]

—Rolling Stone, *June 20, 2017*

A STREAMING RECORD

Drake released *More Life* on March 18, 2017. It became the most-streamed album on any streaming service in a single day. There were a total of 89.9 million streams on Apple Music alone. The album also picked up 61.3 million streams on Spotify. Fans' top three favorites were "Free Smoke," "Portland," and "Passionfruit."[7]

Aside from breaking records, Drake has had a huge impact on the world of hip-hop and the music industry in general. He proved that a biracial Jewish boy with big dreams could start out as a child actor and transform into one of the most successful singers in the music business. That same boy could turn heads in the fashion industry and co-create some of the most sought-after sneaker and jacket designs in retail.

Of course, Drake's rise to fame has not been without controversy—or hardship. The singer has yet to find lasting love. His tendency to get into arguments with a roster of equally outspoken

> **Drake is looking forward to a bright future as his star continues to rise.**

artists over women and fame—Chris Brown to name just one—does not seem to be waning. Still, it seems that Drake has plenty of love to go around—for his fans and for his music.

So what's next for the megastar? A new mixtape? His next studio album and tour dates on the books? More clothing collaborations for OVO? Time will tell. But as always, Drake is cautiously confident and thinking one step ahead about what is to come. "It's about the experience," he says. "If the city isn't talking about it five, six, seven days later, or if people don't remember it for years to come, then I haven't done my job. . . . I'm going to find out what comes after this, but there's definitely another evolution of Drake."[8]

TIMELINE

1986

On October 24, Aubrey Drake Graham is born in Toronto, Ontario, Canada.

2001

Drake lands the role of Jimmy Brooks on the hit teen show *Degrassi: The Next Generation*, and he drops out of high school.

2002

The *Degrassi: The Next Generation* cast wins a Young Artist Award for Best Ensemble in a TV series (Comedy or Drama).

2006

Drake posts a musician profile on MySpace; he releases his first mixtape, *Room for Improvement*.

2007

On September 1, Drake's second mixtape, *Comeback Season*, is released.

2008

On November 18, Lil Wayne and Drake meet for the first time; toward the end of the year, Drake leaves *Degrassi* to pursue his music career.

2009

In February, Drake's third mixtape, *So Far Gone*, is released; Drake is injured while on the America's Most Wanted tour with Lil Wayne.

2010

On June 15, Drake's first studio album, *Thank Me Later*, is released.

2011

On November 15, Drake's second studio album, *Take Care*, is released.

2012

Drake graduates from high school; he lands a role as the voice of Ethan in *Ice Age: Continental Drift* and creates his own record label, OVO Sound.

2013

On September 24, Drake's third studio album, *Nothing Was the Same*, is released; Drake wins his first Grammy—Best Rap Album for *Take Care*.

2014

On January 18, Drake hosts *Saturday Night Live* for the first time.

2015

On February 13, the mixtape *If You're Reading This It's Too Late* is released; on September 20, Drake's joint mixtape with Future, *What a Time to Be Alive*, is released; Drake also lands a $19 million deal with Apple Music to host OVO Sound Radio.

2016

On April 29, Drake's fourth studio album, *Views*, is released; "One Dance" becomes Drake's first solo Number 1 single.

2017

On March 18, Drake's fifth studio album, *More Life*, is released; he makes Number 5 on *Forbes* magazine's annual list of the world's wealthiest hip-hop artists and breaks the record for the most *Billboard* Music Awards in one year, at 13.

FULL NAME
Aubrey Drake Graham

DATE OF BIRTH
October 24, 1986

PLACE OF BIRTH
Toronto, Ontario, Canada

PARENTS
Sandi Graham and Dennis Graham

EDUCATION
Forest Hill Collegiate Institute; Vaughan Road Academy

CAREER HIGHLIGHTS
Drake started his music career in a roundabout way—by appearing on Canada's hit teen soap opera, *Degrassi: The Next Generation*, as jock Jimmy Brooks, from 2001 to 2009. But since releasing his first mixtape in 2006, Drake's hip-hop career has gone only upward. He won his first Grammy in 2013, Best Rap Album, for *Take Care*. He picked up two more in 2017—Best Rap Song and Best Rap/Sung Performance—for "Hotline Bling." He has also made inroads in areas outside of music, including becoming a spokesperson for the Toronto Raptors, founding a record label called OVO Sound, and collaborating on clothing lines with Canada Roots and Nike. In 2017, Drake picked up 13 *Billboard* Music Awards, breaking the previous record of 12 awards in one year, held by Adele.

ALBUMS

Thank Me Later (2010), *Take Care* (2011), *Nothing Was the Same* (2013), *Views* (2016), *More Life* (2017)

CONTRIBUTION TO HIP-HOP

In less than a decade, Drake has taken the music world by storm. As one of the top hip-hop artists in the world, he has influenced the way musicians combine instrumentals, beats, and poetry to create catchy music with strong rhythms. He also proved that singing and rapping could work together in perfect harmony, and he brought back the mixtape as an acceptable way to introduce music to the masses.

CONFLICTS

Drake has had his fair share of serious conflicts, including a bar brawl with Chris Brown over Rihanna and a lawsuit from ex-girlfriend Ericka Lee over lyrics. In more superficial matters, he has also been criticized for wearing excessively expensive clothing and hiding the juicy details of his love life from his adoring fans.

QUOTE

"Live without pretending, Love without depending, Listen without defending, Speak without offending."

—Drake

GLOSSARY

ADVERSITY
Difficult circumstances.

AGENT
A person who helps actors land professional acting jobs.

DEBUT
The first album or publication by a musician or group.

DISTRIBUTION
Delivering or giving something, like an album, to people or businesses.

FORTUITOUS
Fortunate; having or showing good luck.

HOMAGE
Something that is done to honor someone or something.

INSATIABLE
Always wanting more; never satisfied.

LIMELIGHT
Fame or lots of attention, usually because of fame.

LUCRATIVE
Producing a large profit.

PIVOTAL
Very important; life changing.

PLATINUM

An award, given by the Recording Industry Association of America (RIAA), that represents huge sales—500,000 albums for gold, 1 million for platinum, and 2 million or more for multiplatinum.

PREJUDICE

An unfair feeling of dislike for a person or group because of race, sex, or religion.

RAP

A type of music in which words are recited quickly and rhythmically, often over an electronic, prerecorded backing.

RAUCOUS

Uproarious; behaving in a loud, zany way.

REMIX

A new and different version of a previous recording.

ROYALTY

A share of money generated by sales of a work.

SESSION DRUMMER

A musician that is hired to play as part of a backup band but is not a permanent member of that band.

SHOWRUNNER

The person who manages and makes creative decisions for a TV show.

SELECTED BIBLIOGRAPHY

Neyfakh, Leon. "Peak Drake." *FADER*. FADER, 24 Sept. 2015. Web. 23 June 2017.

Paterniti, Michael. "How to Drake It in America." *GQ*. Condé Nast, 18 June 2013. Web. 23 June 2017.

Weiner, Jonah. "Drake: High Times at the YOLO Estate." *Rolling Stone*. Rolling Stone, 13 Feb. 2014. Web. 23 June 2017.

FURTHER READINGS

Cummings, Judy Dodge. *The Men of Hip-Hop*. Minneapolis, MN: Abdo, 2018. Print.

Herringshaw, Deann. *Rihanna*. Minneapolis, MN: Abdo, 2014. Print.

Wittekind, Erika. *Lil Wayne*. Minneapolis, MN: Abdo, 2014. Print.

ONLINE RESOURCES

Booklinks
NONFICTION NETWORK
FREE! ONLINE NONFICTION RESOURCES

To learn more about Drake, visit **abdobooklinks.com**. These links are routinely monitored and updated to provide the most current information available.

MORE INFORMATION

For more information on this subject, contact or visit the following organizations:

GRAMMY MUSEUM
800 W. Olympic Boulevard
Los Angeles, CA 90015-1300
213-765-6800
grammymuseum.org

Founded in 2008, this museum in downtown Los Angeles has exhibits on four floors that cover many aspects of the music business, including the recording process and the history of the Grammy Awards. It also features rotating exhibits about famous musicians.

HIP HOP HALL OF FAME
New York, NY
hiphophof.tv

This online museum explores the latest and greatest hip-hop artists. The website includes photos, videos, a magazine, message boards, and more. A physical museum in New York City is scheduled to open in 2018 and will feature a store, restaurant, concert venue, and rotating exhibits.

NATIONAL MUSEUM OF HIP-HOP
244 Fifth Avenue, Suite 1255
New York, NY 10001
hiphopmuseum.org

The National Museum of Hip-Hop (NMoH) is dedicated to the preservation of hip-hop culture. Founded in 2006, it is the first state-chartered museum dedicated to hip-hop culture and is sanctioned by the New York Board of Education.

SOURCE NOTES

CHAPTER 1. MEETING WEEZY

1. Zara Golden. "The Untold Story of How Drake Met Lil Wayne." *Fader*. Fader, 11 June 2015. Web. 9 Sept. 2017.
2. "Drake Talks Young Money, Kanye Comparisons & Ghostwriting." *Complex*. Complex, 29 May 2009. Web. 9 Sept. 2017.
3. Erika Ramirez. "Lil Wayne's Top 10 Biggest Career Moments." *Billboard*. Billboard, 25 Mar. 2013. Web. 9 Sept. 2017.
4. Zara Golden. "The Untold Story of How Drake Met Lil Wayne." *Fader*. Fader, 11 June 2015. Web. 9 Sept. 2017.
5. Ibid.
6. "Drake — Obey Your Thirst (Episode 1)." *YouTube*. YouTube, 24 June 2015. Web. 9 Sept. 2017.
7. Natalie Robehmed. "Drake's Net Worth: $90 Million In 2017." *Forbes*. Forbes, 12 May 2017. Web. 9 Sept. 2017.
8. Zara Golden. "The Untold Story of How Drake Met Lil Wayne." *Fader*. Fader, 11 June 2015. Web. 9 Sept. 2017.
9. Jon Caramanica. "Review: On Drake's 'More Life,' the Creator Meets the Curator." *New York Times*. New York Times, 20 Mar. 2017. Web. 9 Sept. 2017.
10. "Forbes Five: The Richest in Hip-Hop of 2017." *Forbes*. Forbes, n.d. Web. 9 Sept. 2017.

CHAPTER 2. CANADIAN ROOTS

1. Jonah Weiner. "Drake: High Times at the YOLO Estate." *Rolling Stone*. Rolling Stone, 13 Feb. 2014. Web. 9 Sept. 2017.
2. Jason MacNeil. "Drake Talks Tough Childhood, Juno's Shut-Out, Media Hate to CBC's Q (VIDEO)." *Huffington Post*. Huffington Post, 17 Oct. 2013. Web. 9 Sept. 2017.
3. Damien Scott. "Cover Story Uncut: Drake Talks about Romance, Rap, and What's Really Real." *Complex*. Complex, 15 Nov. 2011. Web. 9 Sept. 2017.
4. Ryan Pfeffer. "Drake's Competition in 2017 Might Just Be His Father." *Billboard*. Billboard, 30 Jan. 2017. Web. 9 Sept. 2017.
5. "Drake." *Biography*. A&E Television Network, n.d. Web. 9 Sept. 2017.
6. Ryan Pfeffer. "Drake's Competition in 2017 Might Just Be His Father." *Billboard*. Billboard, 30 Jan. 2017. Web. 9 Sept. 2017.
7. Harrison Jordan. "*Degrassi* Actor Says Being Different Makes Him Stronger." *InterfaithFamily*. InterfaithFamily, 21 Dec. 2006. Web. 9 Sept. 2017.
8. "Drake." *Biography*. A&E Television Network, n.d. Web. 9 Sept. 2017.

CHAPTER 3. *DEGRASSI: THE NEXT GENERATION*

1. Kadeen Griffiths. "9 Drake Lyrics about 'Degrassi' Because He's Never Forgotten His Acting Roots." *Bustle*. Bustle, 12 Mar. 2015. Web. 9 Sept. 2017.
2. Andres Tardio. "Drake's Woes Also Includes His High School Teacher: See the Pic." *MTV*. Viacom International, 3 June 2015. Web. 9 Sept. 2017.
3. Gil Kaufman. "Drake's High School Diploma: 'One of the Greatest Feelings in My Entire Life.'" *MTV*. Viacom International, 18 Oct. 2012. Web. 9 Sept. 2017.
4. Kadeen Griffiths. "9 Drake Lyrics about 'Degrassi' Because He's Never Forgotten His Acting Roots." *Bustle*. Bustle, 12 Mar. 2015. Web. 9 Sept. 2017.
5. Ibid.
6. Jonah Weiner. "Drake: High Times at the YOLO Estate." *Rolling Stone*. Rolling Stone, 13 Feb. 2014. Web. 9 Sept. 2017.

7. "Drake." *Biography*. A&E Television Network, n.d. Web. 9 Sept. 2017.

8. Ishmael N. Daro. "The Co-Creator of "Degrassi' Says Drake Was Not Actually Kicked Off the Show." *BuzzFeed*. BuzzFeed, 16 Oct. 2015. Web. 9 Sept. 2017.

CHAPTER 4. BREAKOUT SUCCESS

1. Zara Golden. "The Untold Story of How Drake Met Lil Wayne." *Fader*. Fader, 11 June 2015. Web. 9 Sept. 2017.

2. Mariel Concepcion. "Drake's Major Label Bidding War Heats Up, Universal Signing Likely." *Billboard*. Billboard, 3 June 2009. Web. 9 Sept. 2017.

3. Keith Caulfield. "Drake Debuts at No. 1 on Billboard 200." *Billboard*. Billboard, 23 June 2010. Web. 9 Sept. 2017.

4. Mariel Concepcion. "Drake's Major Label Bidding War Heats Up, Universal Signing Likely." *Billboard*. Billboard, 3 June 2009. Web. 9 Sept. 2017.

5. Toshitaka Kondo and Insanul Ahmed. "The Making of Drake's 'Thank Me Later.'" *Complex*. Complex, 9 June 2010. Web. 9 Sept. 2017.

6. Mariel Concepcion. "Drake Signs to Young Money, Distribution by Universal Republic." *Billboard*. Billboard, 30 June 2009. Web. 23 June 2017.

7. Shaheem Reid. "Drake Blogs While Recovering from Knee Injury." *MTV*. Viacom International, 3 Aug. 2009. Web. 9 Sept. 2017.

8. Ben Rayner. "Drake Shoulders the Weight of Great Expectations." *Star*. Toronto Star Newspapers, 14 June 2010. Web. 9 Sept. 2017.

CHAPTER 5. LOVE AND CONFLICT

1. Sasha Frere-Jones. "The Fame Monster." *New Yorker*. Condé Nast, 5 Dec. 2011. Web. 9 Sept. 2017.

2. Greg Kot. "Album Review: Drake, 'Take Care.'" *Chicago Tribune*. Tribune, 13 Nov. 2011. Web. 9 Sept. 2017.

3. "Cash Kings 2012: Hip-Hop's 20 Top Earners." *Forbes*. Forbes, n.d. Web. 9 Sept. 2017.

4. "2012 Pollstar Mid Year Top 50 Worldwide Tours." *Pollstar*. Pollstar, n.d. Web. 9 Sept. 2017.

5. "Drake." *Twitter*. Twitter, 20 Feb. 2011. Web. 9 Sept. 2017.

6. Eriq Gardner. "Drake Beats Lawsuit Over Sampling with Winning 'Fair Use' Argument." *Hollywood Reporter*. Billboard, 31 May 2017. Web. 9 Sept. 2017.

7. Jeremy Gordon. "Drake Pays $100,000 to Rappin' 4-Tay for Ripping Off 'Playaz Club' Lyrics on YG's 'Who Do You Love.'" *Pitchfork*. Condé Nast, 16 July 2014. Web. 23 June 2017.

8. Grace Gavilanes. "A Comprehensive Timeline of Drake & Rihanna's Complicated, Confusing, Adorable Relationship." *People*. Time, 22 Feb. 2017. Web. 9 Sept. 2017.

SOURCE NOTES

CHAPTER 6. RISING TO THE TOP

1. Michael Paterniti. "How to Drake It in America." *GQ*. Condé Nast, 18 June 2013. Web. 9 Sept. 2017.

2. Ibid.

3. Breeanna Hare. "Drake Wins on 'Saturday Night Live.'" *CNN*. Turner Broadcasting, 20 Jan. 2014. Web. 9 Sept. 2017.

4. Michael Paterniti. "How to Drake It in America." *GQ*. Condé Nast, 18 June 2013. Web. 9 Sept. 2017.

5. Ibid.

6. Keith Caulfield. "Drake's 'If You're Reading This' Becomes First Million-Selling Album Released in 2015." *Billboard*. Billboard, 10 Aug. 2015. Web. 9 Sept. 2017.

7. Keith Caulfield. "Drake's 'Nothing Was the Same' Debuts at No. 1 on Billboard 200." *Billboard*. Billboard, 1 Oct. 2013. Web. 9 Sept. 2017.

8. James Vincent. "Drake and Future Release 11-Track Mixtape *What a Time To Be Alive*." *Verge*. Vox, 21 Sept. 2015. Web. 9 Sept. 2017.

9. Latifah Muhammad. "Artist Kadir Nelson Explains Drake's *Nothing Was the Same* Cover." *BET*. Black Entertainment Television, 23 Aug. 2013. Web. 9 Sept. 2017.

10. Ray Waddell. "Live Music's $20 Billion Year: Rolling Stones, One Direction, Live Nation Top Boxscore's Year-End." *Billboard*. Billboard, 12 Dec. 2014. Web. 9 Sept. 2017.

11. Saeed Saeed. "Drake at the Peak of His Powers During Dubai Concert." *National*. International Media Investments, 15 Mar. 2015. Web. 9 Sept. 2017.

CHAPTER 7. NEW ARTISTIC VENTURES

1. Don Reisinger. "Drake's Apple Music Partnership Is a Blockbuster." *Fortune*. Time, 9 May 2016. Web. 9 Sept. 2017.

2. "Revealed: Our Most Stylish Men Alive in 2016 Covers." *GQ*. Condé Nast, n.d. Web. 9 Sept. 2017.

3. Keith Caulfield. "Drake's 'Views' Debuts at No. 1 on Billboard 200 Chart, Sets Streaming Record." *Billboard*. Billboard, 8 May 2016. Web. 9 Sept. 2017.

4. Jayson Greene. "Best New Track: Drake 'Hotline Bling.'" *Pitchfork*. Condé Nast, 5 Aug. 2015. Web. 9 Sept. 2017.

5. Keith Caulfield. "Drake's 'Views' Debuts at No. 1 on Billboard 200 Chart, Sets Streaming Record." *Billboard*. Billboard, 8 May 2016. Web. 9 Sept. 2017.

6. Peacock Roy and Brad Kim. "Hotline Bling." *Know Your Meme*. Literally Media, n.d. Web. 9 Sept. 2017.

7. Colin Stutz. "Drake's 'One Dance' Is Spotify's Most-Streamed Song Ever." *Billboard*. Billboard, 18 Oct. 2016. Web. 9 Sept. 2017.

8. Gregory Babcock. "How the OVO Clothing Label Evolved with Drake's Career." *Complex*. Complex, 15 Oct. 2015. Web. 9 Sept. 2017.

9. "Sotheby's Auctioneer: Drake Was One of the 'Easiest Curators I've Worked with By Far.'" *Fader*. Fader, 30 Apr. 2015. Web. 9 Sept. 2017.

10. Leon Neyfakh. "Peak Drake." *Fader*. Fader, 24 Sept. 2015. Web. 23 June 2017.

11. Rebecca Haithcoat. "Review: Drake Started from the Bottom, Now He's Lonely at the Top on 'Views.'" *SPIN*. Billboard-Hollywood Reporter, 3 May 2016. Web. 9 Sept. 2017.

12. J'na Jefferson. "Drake 'Doesn't Want' His 2017 Grammys, 'Feels Weird' about Category Wins." *VIBE*. Billboard-Hollywood Reporter, 20 Feb. 2017. Web. 9 Sept. 2017.

CHAPTER 8. BREAKING RECORDS

1. "3 Awesome Facts about the Bellagio Fountains." We Las Vegas. Koer Media, 29 Mar. 2017. Web. 9 Sept. 2017.

2. Brianne Tracy. "Prince Michael Jackson Presents Top Billboard Award: 'I'm Honored to Be Here on a Show That Meant So Much to My Father.'" *People*. Time, 21 May 2017. Web. 9 Sept. 2017.

3. "50 Best Albums of 2017 So Far." *Rolling Stone*. Rolling Stone, 20 June 2017. Web. 9 Sept. 2017.

4. Lisa Respers France. "Billboard Music Awards 2017: What You Missed." *CNN*. Turner Broadcasting, 22 May 2017. Web. 9 Sept. 2017.

5. Dan Rys. "Watch Drake Dazzle with a Fiery Performance of 'Gyalchester' Inside a Fountain at the 2017 Billboard Music Awards." *Billboard*. Billboard, 21 May 2017. Web. 17 Oct. 2017.

6. "Drake." *Drake Official*. Drake Official, n.d. Web. 9 Sept. 2017.

7. Micah Singleton. "Drake's *More Life* Shatters Streaming Records with 89.9 Million Streams on Apple Music in 24 Hours." *Verge*. Vox, 20 Mar. 2017. Web. 9 Sept. 2017.

8. Dan Rys. "Drake Sets Single-Year Record, Celine Dion & Cher Shine at 2017 Billboard Music Awards." *Billboard*. Billboard, 21 May 2017. Web. 9 Sept. 2017.

ABOUT THE AUTHOR

Alexis Burling has written dozens of articles and books for young readers on a variety of topics including current events, nutrition and fitness, careers, and biographies of famous writers, musicians, and artists. She is also a book critic with reviews and interviews published in the *New York Times, San Francisco Chronicle,* and more. She lives with her husband in the gorgeous and mountainous Pacific Northwest.